I0163869

The American Holiness Movement: A Bibliographic Introduction

by

Donald Dayton

Occasional Bibliographic Papers of the B.L. Fisher

Library #1

First Fruits Press
Wilmore, Kentucky
c2012

asburyseminary.edu
800.2ASBURY
204 North Lexington Avenue
Wilmore, Kentucky 40390

First Fruits
THE ACADEMIC OPEN PRESS OF ASBURY SEMINARY

ISBN: 9780984738656

The American Holiness Movement: A Bibliographic Introduction, by Donald
W. Dayton.
First Fruits Press, © 2012
B. L. Fisher Library, Asbury Theological Seminary, © 1971

Digital version at http://place.asburyseminary.edu/firstfruitspapers/3/

First Fruits Press is a digital imprint of the Asbury Theological Seminary, B.L.
Fisher Library. Asbury Theological Seminary is the legal owner of the material
previously published by the Pentecostal Publishing Co. and reserves the right to
release new editions of this material as well as new material produced by
Asbury Theological Seminary. Its publications are available for noncommercial
and educational uses, such as research, teaching and private study. First Fruits
Press has licensed the digital version of this work under the Creative Commons
Attribution Noncommercial 3.0 United States License. To view a copy of this
license, visit http://creativecommons.org/licenses/by-nc/3.0/us/.

For all other uses, contact:

First Fruits Press
B.L. Fisher Library
Asbury Theological Seminary
204 N. Lexington Ave.
Wilmore, KY 40390
http://place.asburyseminary.edu/firstfruits

Dayton, Donald W.
    The American Holiness Movement : a bibliographic introduction / by Donald
    Dayton.
    Wilmore, Ky. : First Fruits Press, c2012.
    63 p. ; 21 cm. -- (Occasional bibliographic papers of the B. L. Fisher Library ;
    no. 1)
    Reprint. Previously published: Wilmore, Ky. : B.L. Fisher Library, Asbury
    Theological Seminary, c1971.
    ISBN 9780984738656 (pbk.)
    1. Holiness churches -- United States. 2. Holiness churches -- Bibliography. I. Title.
    II. B. L. Fisher Library. Occasional papers ; no. 1.
Z7845.H6 D3 2012

Cover design by Haley Hill

asburyseminary.edu
800.2ASBURY
204 North Lexington Avenue
Wilmore, Kentucky 40390

First Fruits
THE ACADEMIC OPEN PRESS OF ASBURY SEMINARY

THE AMERICAN HOLINESS MOVEMENT

A BIBLIOGRAPHIC INTRODUCTION

THE AMERICAN HOLINESS MOVEMENT

A BIBLIOGRAPHIC INTRODUCTION

by

Donald W. Dayton

The First in a Series of
"Occasional Bibliographic Papers
of the B.L. Fisher Library"

B.L. Fisher Library
Asbury Theological Seminary
Wilmore, Kentucky 40390
1971

Originally Published in the
1971 PROCEEDINGS of the American
Theological Library Association

All rights reserved by the
Association

Price

1 - 4 copies	$2.00 each
5 or more copies	$1.50 each

plus postage and handling
unless payment accompanies order.

Preface

This paper was first presented to the twenty-fifth
annual conference of the American Theological
Library Association in June, 1971. Each year the
Association attempts to provide a bibliographic
paper relating to the theological tradition of the
institution at which the annual conference is held.
This paper is then printed in the PROCEEDINGS of
the Association and serves as a guide for library
acquisitions in the member schools.

The 1971 Conference was held at Pasadena College,
Pasadena, California, a denominational college of
the Church of the Nazarene. Dr Genevieve Kelly,
then vice-president and program chairman of the
Association, requested a paper on the American
Holiness Movement. Since so little has been done
in this area, I prepared a paper of broader orientation than some in the series in the hope that it
could also serve to introduce others to this
neglected facet of the American Church. A number
of those present at the Conference requested that
the paper be made available to a wider readership
than that of the PROCEEDINGS of the Association.
This booklet is presented in response to those
requests. No attempt has been made to revise the
paper. Only minor, and primarily stylistic,
changes have been made. Local references and the
oral style have been retained.

The library faculty of the B.L. Fisher Library
hope that this paper will be only the first in a
series of "Occasional Bibliographic Papers of the
B.L. Fisher Library." Such papers would present
in similar format other bibliographic projects of
faculty and friends of Asbury Theological Seminary.

I would like to express appreciation to the Rev.
David J Wartluft, executive secretary of the

American Theological Library Association, for
granting permission to reprint this paper from the
PROCEEDINGS; to Mrs. Esther Richter, the library
secretary-receptionist, who typed two drafts of
this paper from a difficult manuscript; to Mrs.
Robert Lyon who prepared the final copy for printing; and especially to Mr. Frank Dewey, my student
assistant, who checked all the references and did
much of the proofreading. I take all responsi-
bility for any errors and would be pleased to be
informed of any that are noticed.

Donald W. Dayton
Acquisitions Librarian and
   Assistant Professor of
   Bibliography and Research
B.L. Fisher Library
Asbury Theological Seminary

Contents

The American Holiness Movement:
A Bibliographic Introduction

Toward a Definition

Before I can introduce you "bibliographically" to
the American Holiness Movement, I must propose
some sort of definition. For some time it
appeared that you might not have this paper because of my inability to clear this first hurdle.
Here we are not dealing with a single denomination
or even with a precisely delimited tradition. The
picture is infinitely more complex. Let me strive
for an adequate definition by first presenting a
short sketch of the main thrust of the movement,
then by indicating some of the variations, and
finally by contrasting this resulting picture with
related movements.

Most of us have at least some awareness of the
turmoil on the American scene during the first
half of the 19th century and of the rise in the
churches of perfectionism, abolitionism, revivalism, etc. Out of this we wish to pick up one
thread. In the 1830's two sisters, Sarah Lankford
and Phoebe Palmer, members of New York City
Methodist churches, organized a weekly prayer
meeting which lasted into the 1900's and became
widely known as the "Tuesday Meeting. This meeting became a center of revival within Methodism
(and to some extent beyond the limits of this
denomination) of the original Wesleyan teaching of
sanctification as a second crisis in the Christian
life in which the believer gained victory over sin.
Phoebe Palmer left her own distinctive cast on this
doctrine by emphasizing that all Christians should

immediately enter into this experience.

In the late 1850's and the following decades, as a part of the general revival of that period,[1] there was a "holiness revival" inspired and fired by the "Tuesday Meeting" and other similar groups. In the late 1860's was founded a "National Camp Meeting Association for the Promotion of Holiness" which evolved over the years into the National Holiness Association (NHA) just renamed in April the Christian Holiness Association (CHA) Toward the end of the last century this movement came more and more into conflict with Methodist leadership. Out of many small groups and state "holiness" association that had grown up, there evolved, usually by a complex series of mergers, separate

---

1. J. Edwin Orr has proposed that we speak of a "Second Evangelical Awakening" in 1857-59 that had such world-wide impact over the next 50 years that it may be compared with the 18th century awakening. If this thesis can be substantiated, then the American Holiness Movement would be that part of this awakening that operated within a "Wesleyan" context. Orr's thesis is defended in his Oxford doctoral dissertation published as THE SECOND EVANGELICAL AWAKENING IN BRITAIN (London: Marshall, Morgan & Scott, 1948) and also in his Northern Baptist Th.D. dissertation published as THE SECOND EVANGELICAL AWAKENING IN AMERICA (London: ?, 1953) These are summarized and popularized in THE SECOND EVANGELICAL AWAKENING (London: Marshall, Morgan & Scott, 1955) More accessible is his THE LIGHT OF THE NATIONS: EVANGELICAL RENEWAL AND ADVANCE IN THE NINETEENTH CENTURY (Grand Rapids: Eerdmans, 1965) which is more general and gives less attention to the development of this particular thesis.

holiness denominations such as the Church of the Nazarene[2] and the Pilgrim Holiness Church.[3] The implications of this growing split are not yet entirely realized. We must, therefore, speak of a movement still in process, but at least for the moment we will describe the American holiness movement as a loosely connected group both within and without Methodism that holds to a primitive Wesleyan position of "second blessing" holiness as shaped on the American scene by such forces as the

---

2. This sequence of events is chronicled in Charles Edwin Jones, "Perfectionist Persuasion: A Social Profile of the National Holiness Movement with American Methodism, 1867-1936." (unpublished Ph.D. dissertation, University of Wisconsin, 1968) Pages 557-567 are an extensive bibliography of materials relating to this denomination. The standard history is now Timothy Smith's excellent CALLED UNTO HOLINESS (Kansas City, Mo.: Nazarene Publishing House, 1962) The Church of the Nazarene has now over a third of a million members and well over twice that in Sunday School enroll-ment (plus another 100,000 overseas)

3. The Pilgrim Holiness Church merged in 1968 with the Wesleyan Methodist Church to form the Wesleyan Church, a denomination now numbering about 82,000 in the U.S.A. and half again as many in the rest of the world. Some account of the history is given in the Jones dissertation (note 2) where pages 571-577 consist of a bibliography relating to the Pilgrim Holiness Church. I am told that a history of the Pilgrims up to merger exists in a manuscript by Paul W. Thomas. A summary history may be found in the final issue of the PILGRIM HOLINESS ADVOCATE (June 29, 1968, incorrectly numbered vol. XLVII #13--actually vol. XLVIII #13)

American camp-meeting and the holiness revival at the time of the Civil War.

This is the main thread, but the stitching is infinitely more complicated. In the first place, at least two denominations presently affiliated with the CHA came into being before the "holiness revival." These arose before the Civil War in the "burned over" district of Western New York State. The Wesleyan Methodist Church[4] was founded in 1842 out of the abolitionist controversy within Methodism, and the Free Methodist Church[5] was founded in

---

4. As mentioned above (note 3) the Wesleyan Methodist Church merged with the Pilgrim Holiness Church in 1968 to form the Wesleyan Church. The history of the Wesleyan branch is chronicled in Roy S. Nicholson's revision (3rd edition) of Ira Ford McLeister's HISTORY OF THE WESLEYAN METHODIST CHURCH OF AMERICA (Marion, Ind.: Wesley Press, 1959) which I understand is being updated by Dr. Nicholson to the time of merger. Other bibliography is given on pages 518-9 of the Jones thesis mentioned previously. It should be noted that the Arno Press of the New York Times has recently reprinted in its series "Anti-Slavery Crusade in America" a book from the controversy surrounding the founding of the Wesleyans: Orange Scott, THE GROUNDS OF SECESSION FROM THE M.E. CHURCH (New York: C. Prindle, 1848; reprinted 1969)

5. This split is justified by B.T. Roberts in WHY ANOTHER SECT (Rochester: "The Earnest Christian" Publishing House, 1879) which consists primarily of response to articles in Bishop Simpson's CYCLOPEDIA OF METHODISM. The standard "interpretive history" of Free Methodism is Bishop Leslie Marston's FROM AGE TO AGE A LIVING WITNESS

1860 when its leaders were expelled from the Genesee Conference of the Methodist Episcopal Church. Both of these groups were then swept more into the holiness orbit during the Holiness Revival.

Secondly, the influence of the Holiness Revival extended far beyond the boundaries of Methodism. Two Mennonite groups, the Missionary Church[6] and the Brethren in Christ,[7] and quite a number of

---

(Winona Lake, Ind.: Light and Life Press, 1960) Other bibliography is provided on pages 568-569 of the Jones thesis. The origins of the denomination are being restudied by James Reinhard of Greenville College (Illinois) for his doctoral program at Iowa. Free Methodists now number about 65,000 in the U.S.A. (nearly double this in Sunday School enrollment) and another 60,000 abroad.

6. The Missionary Church was formed in 1969 by
   union of the Missionary Church Association and the United Missionary Church (formerly the Mennonite Brethren in Christ) There is a small history of the former branch by Walter H. Lugibihl and Jared F Gerig, THE MISSIONARY CHURCH ASSOCIATION (Berne, Ind.: Economy Printing Concern, 1950) The latter branch is treated in an earlier anthology edited by Jasper A. Huffman entitled HISTORY OF THE MENNONITE BRETHREN IN CHRIST CHURCH (New Carlisle, Ohio: Bethel Pub. Co. 1920) There is also a later attempt by Everek Richard Storms, HISTORY OF THE UNITED MISSIONARY CHURCH (Elkhart, Ind.: Bethel Pub. Co. 1958) The new denomination has a membership of about 20,000 members and a Sunday School enrollment of about 40,000.

7   The Brethren in Christ (formerly known as the
    "River Brethren") are popularly known because

"Friends,"[8] were caught up in the Holiness Revival,
adopted Wesleyan views and are now members of the
CHA.   Other groups, such as the Christian and

---

of President Eisenhower's youthful association
with this group. They are closely related to the
groups mentioned in note 6.   There exists a history by Asa W. Climenhaga entitled HISTORY OF THE
BRETHREN IN CHRIST CHURCH (Nappanee, Ind.: E.V.
Pub. House, 1942), but this account has been
called into question at a number of points. See,
for example, "The Origin of the Brethren in Christ
Church and its Later Divisions" by Ira D. Landis
in MENNONITE QUARTERLY REVIEW, XXXIV (October,
1960), 290-307. Carlton O. Wittlinger, Archivist
for the denomination, is, I understand, preparing
a new history. Preliminary studies have appeared
in NOTES AND QUERIES IN BRETHREN IN CHRIST HISTORY,
published by the Archives in Grantham, Pa. The
denomination currently numbers about 10,000 in
American membership and twice that in Sunday School
enrollment.

8.   Four yearly meetings of Friends--Ohio, Rocky
     Mountain, Northwest (formerly Oregon) and
Kansas--have grouped themselves together as the
Evangelical Friends Alliance. All of these have
been influenced by the Holiness Revival but only
the first two of these maintain separate membership in the CHA. Walter R. Williams provides some
of the historical background of these groups in
his THE RICH HERITAGE OF QUAKERISM (Grand Rapids:
Eerdmans, 1962) A few further items of bibliography are given in pages 517-518 of the Jones
thesis (note 2) I am unable to locate statistics
for all of these groups. In 1970 the Ohio Yearly
Meeting reported a membership of about 7,500 and a
Sunday School enrollment of nearly 9,000.

Missionary Alliance[9] show the influence of the movement even though they have never affiliated with CHA.

A third variation may be seen in the Salvation Army. Founder William Booth, a British Methodist, came under the influence of American holiness evangelist James Caughey. This movement came to the U.S.A. in the 1880's and has since identified with the CHA.[10]

---

9. The Christian & Missionary Alliance originated in the 1880's under the leadership of New York City Presbyterian minister A.B. Simpson out of his concern for missions and the disenfranchised. The founder's life has been chronicled by A.E. Thompson, A.B. SIMPSON: HIS LIFE AND WORK (Rev. ed., Harrisburg, Pa.: Christian Publications, 1939) Some historical information is also embedded in the interpretative study of Samuel Stoesz, UNDER-STANDING MY CHURCH (Harrisburg, Pa.: Christian Publications, 1968) The 75th anniversary volume is devoted entirely to chronicling the mission works: J.H. Hunter, BESIDE ALL WATERS (Harrisburg, Pa.: Christian Publications, 1964) The latest edition of the MISSIONARY ATLAS (Harrisburg, Pa.: Christian Publications, 1964) is the fourth in a series. The inclusive membership in North America numbered about 120,000 in 1969 while world-wide was about three times that figure.

10. The definitive history of the Salvation Army is, of course, THE HISTORY OF THE SALVATION ARMY (London: Nelson, 1947-) of which 5 volumes are now complete (the first three by Robert Sandall, the last two by Arch Wiggins) Designed for popular consumption, but centering on the work of the Army in America, is Sallie Chesham, BORN TO BATTLE: THE SALVATION ARMY IN AMERICA (Chicago:

Fourthly, in the basic pattern which produced the Nazarenes and the Pilgrim Holiness Church, there were spawned, especially around the turn of the century - a large number of other groups that have not become affiliated with the CHA. The largest of these is the Church of God (Anderson, Indiana)[11] founded in 1881 by D.S. Warner. They rejected entirely the idea of an organized denomination and withdrew from the national association because of its implicit acceptance of such groups.

And finally certain events in the Twentieth century have produced small off-shoots of Methodism that have identified with the CHA. Among these have been the Evangelical Methodist Church[12]

Rand McNally. 1965) Neither of these gives much attention to the relation of the Salvation Army to the holiness movement. It was in the person of Samuel Logan Brengle, especially at the turn of the century, that this relationship developed. THE YEARBOOK OF AMERICAN CHURCHES (1971) reports inclusive membership of 331,711 for this group.

11. The history of this group has been chronicled at least twice, by Charles E. Brown, WHEN THE TRUMPET SOUNDED: A HISTORY OF THE CHURCH OF GOD REFORMATION MOVEMENT (Anderson, Ind.: Warner Press, 1951) and John W.V. Smith, TRUTH MARCHES ON: A BRIEF STUDY OF THE HISTORY OF THE CHURCH OF GOD REFORMATION MOVEMENT (Anderson, Ind.: Gospel Trumpet Co. 1956) This group reported in 1969 nearly 150,000 members and a Sunday School enrollment of nearly 250,000.

12. There is as yet no major history of this denomination. A short historical sketch was included in the papers of the Study Conference on Federation of Holiness Churches sponsored by the

founded in 1946 in reaction to liberal trends
within Methodism and the Evangelical Church of
North America[13] founded after the 1968 merger of
the Methodist and Evangelical United Brethren
Churches. It will be obvious that different dy-
namics are at work here, but because of their conservative Methodist orientation, these groups
identify with the CHA.

This then is what we shall mean by the American
holiness movement.[14] Total American membership of

NHA in Chicago, Nov. 30 - Dec. 2, 1966. Of some
value is the autobiography of the founder J.H.
Hamblen, A LOOK INTO LIFE (Abilene, Texas: J.H.
Hamblen, 1969)   Current membership is about
10,000.

13. This denomination consists primarily of
     churches from the Evangelical United Brethren,
especially the Pacific Northwest and Montana con-
ferences, as well as churches in the Mississippi
Valley and Western Pennsylvania. It now includes
more than 100 congregations.

14. Other groups both within the CHA and without
     could be mentioned, but the line had to be
drawn somewhere. And of necessity I have used the
present membership of the CHA as a guideline, men-
tioning only the largest and most significant
groups outside. For the sake of completeness I
should include two other small denominations that
do hold CHA membership. The largest of these,
numbering in 1969 about 8,000 members and twice
that in Sunday School enrollment, is the Churches
of Christ in Christian Union, founded in 1909
although its roots go back to Civil War days.
Little seems to be available about them except THE
CHURCHES OF CHRIST IN CHRISTIAN UNION: HISTORY,

these churches (excluding the Christian and Missionary Alliance) would number about one million, though this number is somewhat deceptive. Rather strict membership requirements and vigorous programs of outreach (especially the Sunday School) mean that the actual constituency is probably twice or more the membership. To this total must be added a significant, but decreasing, number of Methodists who would still identify with Methodist institutions, camp meetings, and churches highly influenced by the holiness movement within Methodism.

Much of the American Holiness Movement is loosely grouped together in the Christian Holiness Association. Unity is found primarily in a common commitment to the Wesleyan view of "full salvation." For the most part the individual groups are young and vigorous and still in the process of moving from sect to church if we may use for convenience, Troeltsch's terms. In the neighborhood of 50 schools and colleges, several with graduate

---

ORGANIZATION, MISSIONS, WHAT WE TEACH (Circleville, Ohio: ?, 196?) The other group is the Holiness Christian Church, originally the Pennsylvania Conference of a larger church by this name which participated in the series of mergers producing the Pilgrim Holiness Church. Many other groups could be considered. These can be discovered and traced by use of Leslie Wilcox and Charles Jones (cf. infra under "Bibliography") and the earlier dissertation by Merrill Gaddis (cf. infra under "History"), as well as Elmer T. Clark, THE SMALL SECTS IN AMERICA (Nashville: Cokesbury Press, 1937) Since W.J. Hollenweger does not distinguish holiness from pentecostal groups, much information will be found in his 10 vol. HANDBUCH DER PFINGSTBEWEGUNG, available from the ATLA Board of Microtext.

programs, are affiliated with the CHA. Of particular interest to this group would be the three
theological seminaries associated with the movement: Asbury Theological Seminary (founded 1923),
the Nazarene Theological Seminary (1945), and
Western Evangelical Seminary (1945) The first
two are accredited members of AATS, the third is
an associate member

Finally. I wish to distinguish the American Holiness Movement from three related movements: the
Keswick Movement, Pentecostalism, and Methodism.

It should be noted first of all that there are in
American thought and history many other expres-
sions of holiness and Christian Perfectionism.
Among these would be especially revivalist Charles
Finney and Asa Mahan within Congregationalism.[15]

---

15. Finney's LECTURES ON REVIVALS OF RELIGION
       (Cambridge: Belknap Press of Harvard U.P.,
1960) exist in a critical edition edited by
William G. McLoughlin. Other works of importance
for the holiness movement that have been kept in
print include his LECTURES ON SYSTEMATIC THEOLOGY
(Grand Rapids: Eerdmans, 1951) and SANCTIFICATION
(London: Christian Literature Crusade, 1950)
There is also an edition of his notes for students
entitled SKELETONS OF A COURSE OF THEOLOGICAL LEC-
TURES ON THEOLOGY (Minneapolis: Bethany Fellowship, 1968) His MEMOIRS have been kept in print
by Revell as the AUTOBIOGRAPHY. Seven volumes of
his sermons were published five years ago as "The
Charles G. Finney Memorial Library" by Kregel.
McLoughlin's introduction to the Lectures suggests
bibliography for the life of Finney (p. XVI, pp.
LVI - LIX, and p. 3) There is a popular "holiness" biography by Aaron Merritt Hills, LIFE OF
CHARLES G. FINNEY (Cincinnati: Office of God's

The Oberlin School and Finney's revival techniques
have had great impact on the development of the
American holiness movement. Others in other denominations either came under the influence of the
Palmers' "Tuesday Meeting" or rose concurrently
with it preaching a similar message. Among these

Revivalist," 1902) Richard Taylor, perhaps the
most prominant holiness theologian today, offered
as his doctoral dissertation at Boston in 1953, a
study entitled "The Doctrine of Sin in the Theology of Charles Grandison Finney." It was Asa
Mahan, however, who was more directly appropriated
by the holiness movement. Mahan worked with the
Wesleyans in some projects. THE BAPTISM OF THE
HOLY GHOST was published by the Palmers and is
available today in reprint from both H.E. Schmul
and Newby Book Room. Schmul has also reprinted in
paperback his MISUNDERSTOOD TEXTS OF SCRIPTURE
EXPLAINED AND ELUCIDATED, AND THE DOCTRINE OF THE
HIGHER LIFE THEREBY VERIFIED and in hardback his
CHRISTIAN PERFECTION. Mahan left two major auto-
biographical statements, the AUTOBIOGRAPHY (London:
T. Woolmer, 1882) and the more devotional OUT OF
DARKNESS, INTO LIGHT (various editions) There is
almost no secondary literature on Mahan. Robert S.
Fletcher's two volume HISTORY OF OBERLIN COLLEGE
(Oberlin: Oberlin College, 1943) is important for
both Finney and Mahan. About 200 pages are
devoted to these men in Vol. II of Benjamin B.
Warfield's fiercely polemical PERFECTIONISM (New
York: Oxford U.P. 1931) These were originally
journal articles and are very important bibliographically in studying the Oberlin School as well
as the other figures about to be mentioned in the
background to the Keswick movement. All of the
essays of interest here except the one on Thomas
Upham have been reissued in one volume by
Presbyterian & Reformed Pub. Co. (1958)

were Congregationalist Thomas Upham,[16] professor
at Bowdoin and the first male to enter the hal-
lowed precincts of the "Tuesday Meeting," Baptist
evangelist A.B. Earle,[17] Quakers David Updegraff
and Dougan Clark,[18] and Presbyterians W.E.
Boardman[19] and R. Pearsall Smith and his wife

---

16.   Thomas C. Upham's PRINCIPLES OF THE INTERIOR
       OR HIDDEN LIFE (Boston: D.S. King, 1843) was
the only title by a non-Methodist in a series of
"Abridged Holiness Classics" published by the
Nazarenes in the 1940's. He is also known for his
life of Madame Guyon, frequently reprinted. These
and other works are analyzed by George Peck, "Dr.
Upham's Works, in THE METHODIST QUARTERLY REVIEW,
XXVIII (1846) 248-265. Warfield devoted over 100
pages to him in Vol. II of the original edition of
PERFECTIONISM (cf. note 15)

17   Author of THE REST OF FAITH (Boston: J.H.
      Earle, 1867) and an autobiography. BRINGING
IN SHEAVES (Boston: J.H. Earle, 1868)

18.   A selection of Updegraff's sermons were pub-
       lished as OLD CORN, OR SERMONS AND ADDRESSES
ON THE SPIRITUAL LIFE (Boston: McDonald and Gill,
1892)   His life story is told by Dougan Clark and
Joseph H. Smith, DAVID B. UPDEGRAFF AND HIS WORK
(Cincinnati: published for Smith by the
"Revivalist, 1895)   Clark of Earlham College
contributed several works to the holiness move-
ment. Among these were THE HOLY GHOST DISPENSA-
TION (Chicago: Assn. of Friends, 1891), THE
THEOLOGY OF HOLINESS (Boston: McDonald & Gill,
1893) and THE OFFICES OF THE HOLY SPIRIT (New
York: George Hughes, 1878)

19.   His works include especially THE HIGHER
       CHRISTIAN LIFE (Boston: Henry Hoyt, 1859)

Hannah Whitall Smith.[20] All of these figures had
an impact on the holiness movement, but their
major impact was felt on what is now called the

---

and his life is narrated by his wife, Mary M.
Boardman, LIFE AND LABORS OF REV. W.E. BOARDMAN
(New York: Appleton, 1886) Warfield gives
attention to the Boardmans in his treatment of the
"Higher Life" Movement (note 15)

20. Robert Pearsall Smith wrote HOLINESS THROUGH
     FAITH (Rev. ed.; New York: Anson D.F.
Randolph & Co., n.d.) among other works, but it
was his Quaker wife, Hannah Whitall Smith, who
produced THE CHRISTIAN'S SECRET OF A HAPPY LIFE
(London: 1875) which the publisher claimed in
1952 had sold over 2 million copies and has been
translated into most major languages. It is avail-
able in several editions from Revell. Moody Press
of Chicago has reprinted in paperback her EVERYDAY
RELIGION (1893) and the GOD OF ALL COMFORT (1906)
She wrote an autobiography, THE UNSELFISHNESS OF
GOD (New York: Revell, 1903) Her son Logan
Pearsall Smith, collected her letters in PHILA-
DELPHIA QUAKER (New York: Harcourt, Brace and Co.,
1950), first published in London as A RELIGIOUS
REBEL (London: Nisbet, 1949) Her granddaughter,
Rachel Strachey published under the pseudonym Ray
Strachey a selection of Hannah Whitall Smith's
papers dealing with various 19th century American
religious sects, RELIGIOUS FANATICISM (London:
Faber & Gwyer, 1928) on which she also based a
novel SHAKEN BY THE WIND (London: Faber & Gwyer,
1927 and New York: Macmillan, 1928) Warfield
gives much space to the Smiths and lists her books
on pp. 510-11 of the original edition of
PERFECTIONISM.

Keswick movement,[21] another "higher life" or victorious life" movement somewhat parallel to the Wesleyan holiness movement, but distinguished from it primarily by its context in Reformed theology and its emphasis on gradual rather than instantaneous sanctification.

We must also distinguish the American Holiness Movement from Pentecostalism.[22] This is not done

---

21. The Keswick Movement arose in England out of the work of Boardman and the Smiths and began about 1874 as a series of conventions. It was brought back to the U.S.A. when Moody invited its speakers to Northfield. The "authorized" history is J.C. Pollock's, THE KESWICK STORY (London: Hodder & Stoughton, 1964) Earlier treatments include Walter B. Sloan, THESE SIXTY YEARS (London: Pickering & Inglis, 1935) and Steven Barabas, SO GREAT SALVATION (Westwood, N.J.: Revell, 1952) The latter is particularly helpful, containing an exposition of the teaching, bibliography. biographical sketches. THE KESWICK CONVENTION and THE KESWICK WEEK carry the annual addresses in Britain. A number of these have been anthologized by Herbert F Stevenson in KESWICK'S AUTHENTIC VOICE (Grand Rapids: Zondervan, 1959) and KESWICK'S TRIUMPHANT VOICE (Grand Rapids: Zondervan, 1963) Ernest R. Sandeen in his exciting ROOTS OF FUNDAMENTALISM (Chicago: U. of Chicago Press, 1970) treats briefly the transfer back to the U.S.A. and the subsequent impact on fundamentalism (pp. 172-181)

22. Pentecostal bibliography is an area worthy of study in its own right. I can only make a few preliminary suggestions. The usual introduction now is John Thomas Nichol, PENTECOSTALISM (New York: Harper & Row, 1966) originally a

in many treatments and is the cause of much con-
fusion. It is true that Pentecostalism arose
about the same time and as a result of some of the
same social and theological forces at the turn of
the century that produced the Nazarenes and the
Pilgrim Holiness Church. A common emphasis on the
work of the Holy Spirit led both to use the term
"pentecostal.' It was common among the Nazarenes,
and at Asbury Seminary founder H.C. Morrison's
paper was called the PENTECOSTAL HERALD. But when
the word came to be associated with the experience
of glossolalia, most holiness groups dropped it.
The holiness movement represented by the CHA has
consistently taken a strong stand against this

---

dissertation at Boston U. Included is a helpful,
classified nine page bibliography. Nils Bloch-
Hoell, THE PENTECOSTAL MOVEMENT (Oslo: Universi-
tetsforlaget, 1964; also available from Allen &
Unwin, London) provides European perspective and
international bibliography in greater detail. The
Catholic treatment by Prudencio Damboriena, S.J ,
TONGUES AS OF FIRE (Washington, D.C.: Corpus
Books, 1969) has been well reviewed in some quar-
ters, but is filled with errors (the names of many
holiness leaders, for example, are misspelled)
The bibliography is also mediocre. Extremely help-
ful is the exegetical study by Frederick Dale
Bruner, A THEOLOGY OF THE HOLY SPIRIT: THE PENTE-
COSTAL EXPERIENCE AND THE NEW TESTAMENT WITNESS
(Grand Rapids: Eerdmans, 1970), originally a
Hamburg dissertation. The appendix contains docu-
ments relating to the development of the doctrine
and an extensive and detailed 25 page bibliography.
Of course, for individuals, denominations, and
world-wide coverage, nothing can match the 10
volume HANDBUCH DER PFINGSTBEWEGUNG by Walter J
Hollenweger, available from the ATLA Board of
Microtext and described in a flyer issued by them.

phenomenon. I would suggest that the term "holiness" be used to describe conservative, revivalistic Wesleyanism and "pentecostal" be used to describe these groups that see the baptism of the Holy Spirit accompanied by the experience of "speaking in tongues. This would make perfect sense out of the name Pentecostal Holiness Church,[23] the group with which Oral Roberts was formerly associated. This group does merge a holiness view of sanctification with a pentecostal view of glossolalia, but not all Pentecostal groups are Wesleyan or holiness in understanding. The Assemblies of God, for example, are more "baptistic."[24] I would also suggest that a

---

23. This group was studied for a 1948 Th.D. at Union in Virginia by Joseph E. Campbell. This subsequently became the "official" history as THE PENTECOSTAL HOLINESS CHURCH 1898-1948 (Franklin Springs, Ga.: Publishing House of the PHC, 1951) The origins were restudied at the University of Georgia (1967) by Harold Vinson Synan, THE PENTECOSTAL MOVEMENT IN THE UNITED STATES, which I understand Eerdmans has recently agreed to publish. Synan views Pentecostalism as a descendent from Methodism through the holiness movement. This reflects the perspective of his own denomination and is probably more true of the South in which his denomination is concentrated and which felt the impact of the holiness revival much later because of the movement's early association with abolitionism.

24. The term and the distinction are used by Klaude Kendrick, THE PROMISE FULFILLED (Springfield, Mo.: Gospel Publishing House, 1961), originally a dissertation in history at the University of Texas (1959) This is a standard history of Pentecostalism in the U.S.A. and

bibliographic paper on the branches of Pentecostalism would be of great value to ATLA members.

Finally I must relate the American Holiness Movement to American Methodism. This is, of course, much more complex. The holiness movement claims to be nothing more than primitive Wesleyanism and the true American successors of Wesley. There is much to support this claim, though it must be qualified because of the great impact on the movement of American revivalism and the camp meeting. For two or three decades the movement was, for the most part, within Methodism. The crisis came in the 1880's and 1890's. Successive splits have diluted the holiness movement within Methodism and strengthened the distinct groups. The gap has consistently widened and can be felt especially at such places as Asbury which tries to serve both groups. Until 1950 there had been only one non-Methodist president of NHA. Since 1950 all presidents have been from groups within the CHA. These trends will probably continue. But there is still a large segment of Methodism which relates to institutions identified with the holiness movement, especially in its more mature contemporary forms. Some have suggested that such forces as Methodism's move toward COCU or the rise of the conservative "Good News" movement in Methodism may produce eventually a large conservative "Wesleyan" church built around the core of the larger of the present holiness churches. Only time will tell, of course, what lies ahead.

---

and features the Assemblies of God. He also treats as "holiness-pentecostal groups the Church of God (Cleveland, Tenn.) and the Church of God in Christ. Kendrick's eleven page bibliography should perhaps be mentioned.

Bibliography

I should perhaps remind you at this point that we
are dealing in many ways with a young movement
that until recently has had neither the time nor
the inclination to produce all the accouterments
of scholarship available in older movements or
denominations. Two of the seminaries are only a
quarter of a century old and the third would date
its major growth from the same period. It is not
possible for me to list and describe the various
time-honored, well-tested and reviewed sources. I
must instead indicate, sometimes informally. where
information is available.

For the earlier periods, of course, one may utilize
the Methodist sources. There has been in this
series a paper by Edward L. Fortney on "The History
and Literature of Methodism," ATLA Proceedings,
VIII (1954), 13-17. Asbury is now participating
in the projected Methodist Union Catalog and we
can anticipate that this will become thereby even
more helpful for study in this area. I should
also refer you to the bibliographies in various
scholarly treatments of the related 19th century
American movements. Exemplary of this type of
material would be the "Critical Essay on the
Sources of Information" in Timothy Smith, REVIVAL-
ISM AND SOCIAL REFORM (New York: Abingdon, 1957)

Little exists of the nature of separate bibliographies devoted specifically to the holiness movement. In October 1958, the NHA issued a small
eight-page, envelope-size "Bibliography on the
Deeper Life" which was intended as an "in-print"
list of "available books which present the doctrine
of the Deeper Christian Life from Arminian-Wesleyan
position." This list had been approved by the 90th
annual conference of the NHA in 1958.

Somewhat less than the title suggests, but still

helpful is the MASTER BIBLIOGRAPHY OF HOLINESS
WORKS (Kansas City, Mo.: Beacon Hill Press, 1965)
This was begun several years ago by Dr. Ross Price
at Pasadena, and was completed over the years at
the Nazarene Theological Seminary with the help of
a number of the faculty there. The NHA Bibliography was incorporated into this forty-five page
booklet containing about 700 titles. These are
divided into two groups, those that "promote
Christian holiness" (Part I) and "those related
treatises which provide suitable breadth in background reading." There is no attempt at classifi-
cation, annotation, or the indication of original
or varying editions. The last I knew this bibliography was available for the asking from the
Nazarene Theological Seminary.

Of more value in many ways, though not as complete,
is Leslie D. Wilcox, BE YE HOLY (Cincinnati: The
Revivalist Press, 1965) This originated as a
mimeographed syllabus for Dean Wilcox's classes at
God's Bible School in Cincinnati, and is now available in the second edition of the book form. This
book is most helpful. The first third consists of
a rather traditional statement of the position,
with its scriptural support and suggested readings
at each point. The other 270 pages are devoted to
history and bibliography of the movement. This
treatment starts with Wesley and puts the whole
movement in that context. Included are thumbnail
sketches of major groups, essays on doctrinal
development, introduction to the controversies
within the movement, etc.

Finally I would like to draw your attention to a
dissertation (already mentioned) by Charles E.
Jones, now of Houghton College, "Perfectionist
Persuasion: A Social Profile of the National
Holiness Movement Within American Methodism, 1867-
1936" (University of Wisconsin, 1968 - University
Microfilms order #68-9083) The degree could have

been awarded merely on the basis of the nearly 300 pages of appended material and bibliography! He includes charts showing denominational origins and inter-relationships, Camp Meeting sites and committees, a fifteen page list of present and past holiness schools with founding dates and all name changes, and one hundred and forty pages of classified bibliography.

It should perhaps be noted that serious bibliographic work on this movement has been available only in the last six years. This paper would have been impossible without these recent efforts.

History

The historian par excellence of the American Holiness Movement is Nazarene Timothy L. Smith of Johns Hopkins. He set the context of the movement in a book based on his Harvard dissertation, REVIVALISM AND SOCIAL REFORM IN MID-NINETEENTH-CENTURY AMERICA (New York: Abingdon, 1957), now a standard work. He picked up the story again in his official history of the Church of the Nazarene, CALLED UNTO HOLINESS (Kansas City, Mo.: Nazarene Publishing House, 1962) Any student of the movement must start with these books and have his path further indicated by the bibliographic treasures embedded in Smith's documentation. A shorter 20 page statement supplementing these accounts may be found in Vol. II of THE HISTORY OF AMERICAN METHODISM (New York: Abingdon, 1964), under the title "The Holiness Crusades" (pp. 608-627)

Three works are of importance in tracing the development of the doctrine of Christian Perfection within American Methodism. Most readily available is John Leland Peters, CHRISTIAN PERFECTION AND AMERICAN METHODISM (New York: Abingdon, 1956), originally a Yale dissertation. To this

must be added two unpublished dissertations. M.E.
Gaddis, "Christian Perfectionism in America"
(Doctoral dissertation, University of Chicago,
1929) moves from New Testament times until the
beginnings of the 20th century. Claude Thompson
of Emory produced "The Witness of American Methodism to the Historical Doctrine of Christian Perfection" (Doctoral dissertation, Drew University,
1949) which sees in Methodism the source of all
modern perfectionist movements.

C.E. Jones, "Perfectionist Persuasion," already
repeatedly cited, indicates further bibliography
on the social context (pp. 521-525) and Methodist
backgrounds (pp. 526-531) Jones chronicles the
events from the 1850's until the rise of the
Church of the Nazarene and the Pilgrim Holiness
Church, giving particular attention to social
forces, and the impact of the camp meeting as an
institution. Delbert Rose of Asbury Seminary provides a short history of the National Holiness
Association as chapter two of his A THEOLOGY OF
CHRISTIAN EXPERIENCE (Minneapolis: Bethany
Fellowship, 1965), originally his Iowa dissertation in 1952 and actually a treatment of the life
and thought of Joseph H. Smith, "A product of the
NHA who became its chief expositor-evangelist."
Use of this work is unfortunately made difficult
by its lack of an index. Rose, the official
historian of the CHA, is working now on the manuscript of the "official history. Also in progress
is a "social history" of the American holiness
movement by Melvin Dieter, General Secretary of
Educational Institutions in the Wesleyan Church,
as a part of his doctoral program at Temple
University.

I have tried to indicate above, in the notes to
the first section, the standard histories of denominations related to the holiness movement.
Jones, "Perfectionist Persuasion," gives extended

references (pp. 556-579)   I have attempted to
supplement this, giving above more detailed information where he is weak. He also provides references to histories of important camp meetings
(pp. 547-550), social agencies and educational
institutions (pp. 550-552) and holiness associa-
tions and interdenominationalism (pp. 552-555)
Special mention should perhaps be made of Percival
Wesche, "The Revival of the Camp-Meeting by the
Holiness Groups" (unpublished M.A. thesis, University of Chicago Divinity School, 1945) and Morris
S. Daniels, THE STORY OF OCEAN GROVE (New York:
Methodist Book Concern, 1919, available on micro-
film from University Microfilms) The history of
Asbury Seminary has been told three times, but the
only published narrative is by Howard F Shipps of
Asbury as A SHORT HISTORY OF ASBURY THEOLOGICAL
SEMINARY (Wilmore, Ky.: Asbury Theological
Seminary. 1953)

Biography

For 19th century figures, the usual Methodist
sources are of much value. A few very early figures like Orange Scott and Timothy Merritt made it
into the Methodist Volume (VII) of the ANNALS OF
THE AMERICAN PULPIT (New York: R. Carter, 1865,
reprinted 1969 by the Arno Press of the New York
Times) edited by William B. Sprague. Of more
value is Bishop Matthew Simpson, CYCLOPEDIA OF
METHODISM (5th edition; Philadelphia: Louis H.
Everts, 1882) Carl Price, WHO'S WHO IN AMERICAN
METHODISM (New York: E.B. Treat, 1916) is still
of help for turn of the century figures. But by
the time Price and Simpson were supplemented by
Clinton T. Howell, PROMINENT PERSONALITIES IN
AMERICAN METHODISM (Birmingham, Ala.: Lowry Press,
1945) only very occasional entries are of inter-
est. Frederick DeLand Leete, METHODIST BISHOPS:
PERSONAL NOTES AND BIBLIOGRAPHY (Nashville:

Parthenon, 1948) is also of value for some 19th century figures.

The later periods are much leaner in sources. Occasionally the standard biographical sources will be of some value for outstanding figures, but one should turn first to Jones, "Perfectionist Persuasion." About 80 pages of his bibliography (pp. 583-660) are devoted to "personalities." For each of nearly 300 figures he lists the standard sources in which biographical information may be found, indicates their own works and notes any separate biographies that may exist. Some of the larger or older holiness denominations have produced anthologies about their leaders or founder. Richard Blews produced an excellent volume on the Free Methodist Bishops under the title MASTER WORKMEN (Winona Lake: Light and Life Press, 1939; centennial edition, 1960) The Nazarenes have produced C.T. Corbett, OUR PIONEER NAZARENES (Kansas City, Mo.: Nazarene Publishing House, 1958) and Basil Miller, OUT UNDER THE STARS: LIFE SKETCHES OF EARLY NAZARENE LEADERS (Kansas City. Mo.: Nazarene Publishing House, 1941)

Individual biographies are of course, numerous. Many are not scholarly, and often the concern is more with piety than history. Some of these have already been indicated. Orange Scott of the Wesleyans was treated in 2 volumes by his comrade in the abolitionist movement, Lucius C. Matlack, LIFE OF ORANGE SCOTT (New York: C. Prindle and L.C. Matlack, 1847-48) B.T. Roberts of the Free Methodists was studied by Clarence H. Zahniser, EARNEST CHRISTIAN (n.p., 1957), based on his dissertation at Pittsburgh, 1951. Shortly after her death in 1874, the life of Phoebe Palmer was published by Richard Wheatley, THE LIFE AND LETTERS OF MRS. PHOEBE PALMER (New York: W.C. Palmer, Jr., 1876) Ernest Wall provides a short and more recent treatment as "I Commend Unto You Phoebe,"

RELIGION IN LIFE, XXVI (Summer, 1957), 396-408.
Dr. W.C. Palmer wrote THE LIFE AND LETTERS OF
LEONIDAS L. HAMLINE D.D. (New York: Carlton and
Porter, 1866) while his life in turn was chron-
icled by George Hughes, THE BELOVED PHYSICIAN,
WALTER C. PALMER (New York: Palmer and Hughes,
1884) The life of John Inskip, president of the
National Holiness Association for its first 17
years, was told by the next president William
McDonald and John E. Searles, "I AM, O LORD,
WHOLLY AND FOREVER THINE," THE LIFE OF REV. JOHN
S. INSKIP (Boston: McDonald and Gill, 1885) We
have already mentioned Delbert Rose's treatment of
later president Joseph H. Smith (cf. supra under
History) The Salvation Army leader in America
has been treated by Clarence Hall, SAMUEL LOGAN
BRENGLE (Chicago: Salvation Army Supply and Pur-
chasing Dept., 1933) a popular holiness biography
which has gone through a number of printings and
is still available. Donald P. Brickley has considered the life and work of Nazarene founder
Phineas F. Bresee in MAN OF THE MORNING (Kansas
City, Mo.: Nazarene Publishing House, 1960), based
on his dissertation at Pittsburgh, 1958. Of the
Pilgrims, Martin Wells Knapp has been considered
by Aaron M. Hills, A HERO OF FAITH AND PRAYER
(Cincinnati: Mrs. M.W. Knapp, 1902) and SETH COOK
REES: THE WARRIOR-SAINT (Indianapolis: Pilgrim
Book Room, 1934) by his son, Paul S. Rees. The
founder of Asbury Theological Seminary was studied
by Percival A. Wesche, HENRY CLAY MORRISON:
CRUSADER SAINT (Berne, Ind.: Herald Press for
Asbury Theological Seminary, 1963), based on his
dissertation at Oklahoma U., 1955.

There is also in the holiness movement a genre of
literature that stands midway between theology and
biography. The holiness evangelist hopes to produce the changed life rather than a system of
doctrine. Theology is embedded in life and taught
by means of biography. autobiography or the

relating of religious experience. Many of the examples cited above fall into this category. But it is the anthologies which are perhaps more interesting. At least two of these were brought out by Phoebe Palmer The best known is probably PIONEER EXPERIENCES: OR THE GIFT OF POWER RECEIVED BY FAITH, ILLUSTRATED AND CONFIRMED BY THE TESTIMONIES OF EIGHTY LIVES: WITNESSES OF VARIOUS DENOMINATIONS (New York: W.C. Palmer, Jr. 1868) HOLINESS MISCELLANY (Philadelphia: National Publishing Assn. for the Promotion of Holiness, 1882) records the "testimonies" of prominent holiness leaders within Methodism. Perhaps the most popular was edited by S. Olin Garrison, FORTY WITNESSES COVERING THE WHOLE RANGE OF CHRISTIAN EXPERIENCE (New York: Hunt & Eaton, 1888) From the 20th century, we have, among others, Bernie Smith, FLAMES OF LIVING FIRE: TESTIMONIES TO THE EXPERIENCE OF ENTIRE SANCTIFICATION (Kansas City, Mo.: Beacon Hill, 1950) Similar, but not personal statements, is Mrs. Clara McLeister, MEN AND WOMEN OF DEEP PIETY (Syracuse: Wesleyan Methodist Publishing Association, 1920 - reprinted 1970 by Newby Book Room) edited and published by well-known holiness evangelist E.E. Shelhamer. Widely read, reprinted, and translated has been James Gilchrist Lawson, DEEPER EXPERIENCES OF FAMOUS CHRISTIANS (Anderson, Ind.: Warner Press, 1911) still available and reprinted in paperback. These last two books draw on the wider Christian tradition to teach holiness lessons.

Theology

Holiness theology also presents a complicated and variegated picture. The Holiness Movement emphasizes the classical Methodist works. Primary of course is John Wesley, A PLAIN ACCOUNT OF CHRISTIAN PERFECTION, consistently reprinted, but in various formats, some of which have been somewhat mutilated.

A holiness collection of Wesley's sermons will usually include "On Sin in Believers" and "The Repentence of Believers" which are not a part of the standard forty-four usually published. Saintly John Fletcher is also to be noted. His CHECKS TO ANTINOMIANISM have been valued, while his essay on "The New Birth" has been frequently reprinted, as well as an extract from his last "Check" as FLETCHER ON PERFECTION. Adam Clarke's famous six volume commentary has been the standard for holiness exegesis and has been abridged recently by Ralph Earle of the Nazarene Seminary into one large volume as Adam Clarke, COMMENTARY ON THE HOLY BIBLE (Kansas City. Mo.: Beacon Hill, 1967) Chapter 12 of his CHRISTIAN THEOLOGY (available in reprint from H.E. Schmul) has often been reprinted as ENTIRE SANCTIFICATION. Richard Watson's THEOLOGI-CAL INSTITUTES is also highly regarded.

Almost all holiness systematic theologies are by Methodist writers. Two British efforts have found much use in the United States. These are William B. Pope A COMPENDIUM OF CHRISTIAN THEOLOGY (2nd Rev. ed.; London: Wesleyan Conference Office, 1877-80) in three volumes and J. Agar Beet, A MANUAL OF THEOLOGY (London: Hodder and Stoughton, 1906 - also New York, 1906) which also appeared in an abridged edition. American Methodism has provided from Vanderbilt, T.O. Summers, SYSTEMATIC THEOLOGY (Nashville: Southern Methodist Publishing House, 1888) and from Drew, Bishop Randolph S. Foster's 6 volume STUDIES IN THEOLOGY (New York: Hunt and Eaton, 1889-99), John Miley's two volume SYSTEMATIC THEOLOGY (New York: Methodist Book Concern, 1894) and Olin Curtis' THE CHRISTIAN FAITH (Cincinnati: Jennings & Graham, 1905) though Miley and Curtis have had mixed reception.[25] Still

---

25. Robert Chiles, THEOLOGICAL TRANSITION IN
    AMERICAN METHODISM: 1790-1935 (New York:

required in some courses of study is the short
volume by Amos Binney and Daniel Steele, BINNEY'S
THEOLOGICAL COMPEND IMPROVED (New York: Nelson
and Phillips, 1875)   In the 19th century Wesleyan
Luther Lee attempted ELEMENTS OF THEOLOGY
(Syracuse: S. Lee, 1856)   Two twentieth century
attempts have been made by Nazarenes A.M. Hills,
FUNDAMENTAL CHRISTIAN THEOLOGY (Pasadena, Calif.:
C.J. Kinne, 1931) in two volumes and H. Orton
Wiley, CHRISTIAN THEOLOGY (Kansas City. Mo.:
Nazarene Publishing House, 1940-1943)   This three
volume work was abridged with Paul T. Culbertson
as INTRODUCTION TO CHRISTIAN THEOLOGY (Kansas City,
Mo.: Beacon Hill, 1947)   Wiley has been standard,
but is cast in a scholastic mode with emphasis on
polemic against 19th century Calvinism. As far as

Abingdon, 1965) is extremely illuminating and most
helpful for tracing the vicissitudes of Methodist
theology on the American scene. He confirms the
reservations of certain holiness thinkers about
these two men by seeing in them a crucial turning
point in American Methodist theology. But as far
as I know Chiles' thesis has not found wide circulation in holiness theological circles, perhaps
because of his somewhat Barthian categories. Also
of help is an essay from within the perspective of
the Evangelical Congregational Church, a split from
within the background of the Evangelical United
Brethren Church. Joel Samuels, now of the Newberry
Library in Chicago, has provided us with a "Bibliography of Wesleyan-Arminian Theology." LIBRARY
BULLETIN (of the Evangelical Congregational School
of Theology), VI (October, 1965) 1-9. Samuels
draws attention to the work of S.J Gamertsfelder,
SYSTEMATIC THEOLOGY (Harrisburg, Pa.: Evangelical
Publishing House, 1919) and others within this
tradition and adds further comments about Miley
and Curtis.

I know, nothing is imminent, and meanwhile the gap
has been partly filled with W.T. Purkiser (ed.)
EXPLORING OUR CHRISTIAN FAITH (Kansas City. Mo.:
Beacon Hill, 1960), an anthology apparently designed as a college text in which essays on various "loci of theology are collected.

But systematics have not been the forte of the
holiness movement. Much more characteristic are
collections of addresses or camp-meeting sermons
and treatises on the doctrine of primary concern
to the movement. Perhaps the first of these of
interest was THE CHRISTIAN'S MANUAL: A TREATISE
ON CHRISTIAN PERFECTION WITH DIRECTIONS FOR OBTAIN-
ING THAT STATE (New York: Carlton & Porter, 1824)
by Timothy Merritt who founded THE GUIDE TO CHRIS-
TIAN PERFECTION. In 1841 George Peck, the editor
of THE QUARTERLY REVIEW, issued the SCRIPTURE
DOCTRINE OF CHRISTIAN PERFECTION (New York: Lane
and Sandford, 1842) Later there appeared a similar work by his brother, Jesse Peck, THE CENTRAL
IDEA OF CHRISTIANITY (Boston: H.V. Degen, 1856
issued in "Abridged Holiness Classic" series by
Beacon Hill, 1951, another shorter form available
in CHRISTIAN PERFECTION, a compilation of six holiness classics in one by H.E. Schmul) Of Phoebe
Palmer's many works should be mentioned the smaller
THE WAY OF HOLINESS (New York: Lane & Tippett,
1845) which went through 51 printings by 1871 and
the larger FAITH AND ITS EFFECTS (New York: Walter
C. Palmer, 1854) From the same period we should
mention LETTERS ON SANCTIFICATION or more properly
THE NECESSITY NATURE AND FRUITS OF SANCTIFICATION
(New York: Lane & Scott, 1851) by Nathan Bangs,
one of the greatest leaders of 19th century
American Methodism.

A number of other Methodists made similar contributions. John A. Wood, who first suggested the
camp meeting association, wrote PERFECT LOVE
(Philadelphia: S.D. Burlock, 1861 - issued in

"Abridged Holiness Classics" series by Beacon
Hill, 1944 and recently reprinted by Newby) and
PURITY AND MATURITY (Boston: Christian Witness
Co., 1899 - issued in "Abridged Holiness Classics"
series by Beacon Hill, 1944)   William McDonald,
second president of the National Campmeeting
Association, contributed among others THE SCRIP-
TURAL VIEWS OF HOLINESS (Philadelphia: National
Publishing Association for the Promotion of Holi-
ness, 1877)   Bishop Randolph Foster produced
CHRISTIAN PURITY (New York: Harper and Brothers,
1851 - issued in the "Abridged Holiness Classics"
series by Beacon Hill, 1944 - another abridged
form now available in CHRISTIAN PERFECTION, six
holiness classics in one, by H.E. Schmul)   Asbury
Lowry who for some time edited THE CHRISTIAN
STANDARD wrote POSSIBILITIES OF GRACE (New York:
Phillips and Hunt, 1884 - issued in the "Abridged
Holiness Classics" series by Beacon Hill, 1944)
Near the turn of the century, Bishop Willard F
Mallalieu contributed THE FULLNESS OF THE BLESSING
OF THE GOSPEL OF CHRIST (Cincinnati: Jennings and
Pye, 1903)   T.O. Summers of Vanderbilt wrote
HOLINESS, A TREATISE ON SANCTIFICATION (Richmond:
J Early 1850)   Perhaps the most significant
contributions were made by Daniel Steele, who
taught at both Syracuse and Boston. His works
have been constantly reprinted and include HALF
HOURS WITH ST. PAUL (Boston: Christian Witness
Co. 1895 - recently reprinted by Schmul), HALF
HOURS WITH ST. JOHN (Chicago: Christian Witness
Co., 1901 - recently reprinted by Schmul), MILE-
STONE PAPERS (New York: Eaton & Mains, 1876, later
enlarged - original edition recently reprinted by
Bethany Fellowship) containing his much referred
to defense of holiness from the Greek tenses, LOVE
ENTHRONED (Boston: Christian Witness Co., 1875 -
recently reprinted by Schmul) JESUS EXULTANT
(Boston: Christian Witness Co. 1899 - recently
reprinted by Schmul) and THE GOSPEL OF THE COMFORT-
ER (Boston: Christian Witness Co., 1897 -

recently reprinted by West Pub. Co. Apollo, Pa.)

Evangelists have also contributed much to the
holiness literature. Beverly Carradine from the
South wrote over twenty full-sized books. His
SECOND BLESSING IN SYMBOL (Columbia, S.C.: L.L.
Picket, 1893 - reprinted by Newby. 1968) illus-
trates the allegorical interpretation into which
holiness evangelists often fell. THE OLD MAN
(Louisville: Pentecostal Publishing Co. 1896 -
reprinted by Newby - 1965) raises in standard camp-
meeting terminology the problem of "inbred sin."
Others of his books deal more directly with sanctification. W.B. Godbey, best known for his COMMEN-
TARY ON THE NEW TESTAMENT (Cincinnati: Revivalist
Office, 1896-1900 and still available), also produced a number of other works including SANCTIFI-
CATION (Louisville: Kentucky Methodist Pub. Co.,
1896) Also an expositor and author of over
twenty books was George Watson, a Methodist who
later turned Wesleyan. Among his works was A
HOLINESS MANUAL (Boston: Christian Witness, Co.
1882) S.A. Keen, asked by Methodist Bishops to
hold services in 76 different annual conference
sessions, produced half a dozen works, among them
FAITH PAPERS (Cincinnati: God's Revivalist, 1888 -
recently reprinted in full in CHRISTIAN PERFECTION,
six holiness classics in one, by H.E. Schmul)
And the list could be indefinitely extended in
terms of both authors and books.

The independent bodies have of course produced a
great deal of material. Free Methodist B.T
Roberts' editorial writings in THE EARNEST CHRIS-
TIAN were compiled by his son Benson H. Roberts
as HOLINESS TEACHINGS (North Chili, N.Y.: Earnest
Christian Pub. House, 1893 - reprinted in paper-
back by Schmul, 1964) Much more recently Bishop
J. Paul Taylor contributed HOLINESS - THE FINISHED
FOUNDATION (Winona Lake, Ind.: Light and Life
Press, 1963 - also reissued in paperback) The

Wesleyans have produced a number of writers, but probably most interesting is Roy S. Nicholson, THE ARMINIAN EMPHASES (Owosso, Michigan: Owosso College, 196-)   Dr. Nicholson was for years General Conference President.   A founder of the Pilgrim Holiness Church and one of the most important figures of the turn of the century was Martin Wells Knapp, author of several books.   Among these was OUT OF EGYPT INTO CANAAN: LESSONS IN SPIRITUAL GEOGRAPHY (Cincinnati: Cranston & Stowe, 1887 - recently reprinted by Book Nook, Box 2434, Phoenix, Arizona), a classical example of "Exodus" typology in holiness thought.   From the Friends we have Everett Cattell of Malone College, THE SPIRIT OF HOLINESS (Grand Rapids: Eerdmans, 1963)   Jasper A. Huffman of the United Missionary Church has produced a large number of books.   Among them REDEMPTION COMPLETED (New Carlisle, Ind.: The Bethel Publishing Co., 1903) has gone through several editions.   A 20th century classic was contributed by Englishman Harry E. Jessop who became Dean of the Chicago Evangelistic Institute (now Vennard College in Iowa)   This widely used text is FOUNDATIONS OF DOCTRINE IN SCRIPTURE AND EXPERIENCE (Chicago: Chicago Evangelistic Institute, 1938 - still available from Vennard College, University Park, Iowa)   Charles E. Brown of the Church of God (Anderson, Ind.) wrote the widely used THE MEANING OF SANCTIFICATION (Anderson, Ind.: The Warner Press, 1945 - recently reissued in paperback)   Commissioner Samuel Logan Brengle of the Salvation Army left among others HELPS TO HOLINESS (New York: Salvation Army. 1918 - still available)

The Nazarenes have been by far the most prolific of the independent groups.   From the 19th century we have the classic by A.M. Hills, originally a congregationalist who studied under Finney   HOLINESS AND POWER (Cincinnati: Revivalist Office, 1897 - still available)   R.T. Williams wrote

SANCTIFICATION: THE EXPERIENCE AND THE ETHICS
(Kansas City, Mo.: Nazarene Publishing House,
1928 - recently reprinted in paper by Schmul)
General Superintendent James B. Chapman's THE
TERMINOLOGY OF HOLINESS (Kansas City, Mo.: Beacon
Hill, 1947 - recently reissued in paperback) has
had wide circulation. A strict view of holiness
doctrine is defended in Stephen S. White, ERADICA-
TION DEFINED, EXPLAINED, AUTHENTICATED (Kansas
City, Mo.: Beacon Hill, 1954 - reissued in paperback) W.T. Purkiser has written two popular
short treatments, CONFLICTING CONCEPTS OF HOLINESS
(Kansas City, Mo.: Beacon Hill, 1953) and SANCTI-
FICATION AND ITS SYNONYMS (Kansas City. Mo.:
Beacon Hill, 1961 - recently reissued in paperback)
These two books are helpful in gaining insight into
contemporary debate. The most outstanding holiness theologian today is no doubt Richard Taylor
of the Nazarene Seminary. His is a somewhat updated, but traditional approach. His most important works are A RIGHT CONCEPTION OF SIN (Kansas
City. Missouri: Nazarene Publishing House, 1939 -
recently reissued in paper), THE DISCIPLINED LIFE
(Kansas City, Mo.: Beacon Hill, 1962 - available
in paper) and LIFE IN THE SPIRIT (Kansas City.
Mo.: Beacon Hill, 1966 - available also in
paper).26

---

26. Much literature has of course risen to attack
     the holiness theology. One of the earliest
of these on the American scene was Samuel Franklin's
A CRITICAL REVIEW OF WESLEYAN PERFECTION (Cincin-
nati: Methodist Book Concern, 1866) Also within
Methodism, but arising out of the controversies
just before the turn of the century were J.M.
Boland, THE PROBLEM OF METHODISM (Nashville:
Printed for the Author by the Publishing House of
the Methodist Episcopal Church, South, 1888) and
James Mudge, GROWTH IN HOLINESS TOWARD PERFECTION,

Periodicals

By its very nature, the Holiness Movement has found
major expression in periodical literature. This
material is just beginning to be studied. Delbert
Rose of Asbury has published a list of over 60
holiness periodicals (mostly discontinued) as
Appendix C (pp. 273-4) of his THEOLOGY OF CHRISTIAN
EXPERIENCE. Appendix C2 (pp. 437-450) of Charles
Jones, "Perfectionist Persuasion" nearly triples
this figure and provides founding dates, title
changes, sponsorship, and cross references from
variant titles. Dr. Rose is continuing his com-
pilations and has added information to both lists,
but nothing is ready yet for further publication.

Perhaps most important was the GUIDE TO CHRISTIAN
PERFECTION founded in Boston in 1839. In 1845 the
title became GUIDE TO HOLINESS. It was purchased
by Dr. W.C. Palmer and moved to New York City
where it was published until 1901. Phoebe Palmer
took over the editing and by 1873 circulation had
reached 40,000.

———————————————

OR PROGRESSIVE SANCTIFICATION (New York: Hunt and
Eaton, 1895) among others. H.A. Ironside, who had
unfortunate experiences with the Salvation Army,
launched a fierce attack in HOLINESS: THE FALSE
AND THE TRUE (New York: Loiseaux Brothers, 1912)
which went through ten printings in the next 30
years. We have already mentioned Benjamin B.
Warfield's PERFECTIONISM which treats most of the
related movements, but does not directly attack
Wesleyan perfectionism. Finally. a short article
by C.T. Craig should be mentioned, "Paradox of
Holiness: New Testament Doctrine of Sanctification," INTERPRETATION, VI (April, 1952) 147-61.
This article attacks the Biblical foundations of
the doctrine.

Out of the National Camp Meeting Association came
in 1876 the CHRISTIAN STANDARD (first published as
the METHODIST HOME JOURNAL) and in 1870 the CHRIS-
TIAN WITNESS (originally the ADVOCATE OF CHRISTIAN
HOLINESS) which ceased publication finally in 1959.
The CHRISTIAN WITNESS is presently being collated
for filming by the ATLA Board of Microtext. From
1948-1957 the STANDARD OF HOLINESS served as the
organ of the NHA and ceased publication so as not
to compete with denominational organs.

Before the turn of the century a number of region-
al holiness association published periodicals.
Among these were the BANNER OF HOLINESS (Western
Holiness Association), THE HIGHWAY (Iowa Holiness
Association), THE GOOD WAY (Southwestern Holiness
Association), MICHIGAN HOLINESS RECORD (Michigan
Holiness Association) and the PACIFIC HERALD OF
HOLINESS (Pacific Coast Holiness Association), etc.

Holiness periodicals also grew up around major
figures and schools. Associated with Martin Wells
Knapp and God's Bible School in Cincinnati was
GOD'S REVIVALIST AND BIBLE ADVOCATE (1888 - date,
before the turn of the century as THE REVIVALIST)
Associated with the Chicago Evangelistic Institute
(now Vennard College of Iowa) was HEART AND LIFE
which was founded in 1911 and ceased publication
in the 1950's. Associated with Henry Clay
Morrison and now with Asbury Theological Seminary
has been the HERALD (published under a variety of
titles but especially the PENTECOSTAL HERALD)
1888 - date.

Several denominational papers have long histories.
The WESLEYAN ADVOCATE dates back through the
WESLEYAN METHODIST to the TRUE WESLEYAN founded in
1843. The FREE METHODIST, recently retitled LIGHT
AND LIFE, dates from 1868. THE GOSPEL TRUMPET,
retitled VITAL CHRISTIANITY in 1963, has served as
the organ of the Church of God (Anderson, Indiana)

since 1881. The NAZARENE MESSENGER (founded in 1896) became the HERALD OF HOLINESS in 1912. The latter title is being collated for filming by the ATLA Board of Microtext. Other denominational periodicals can be located in the standard sources or with the help of the Jones dissertation, "Perfectionist Persuasion.'

Other periodicals have arisen more recently. Since 1941 we have had the AMERICAN HOLINESS JOURNAL published by the West Publishing Company of Apollo, Pa. More recently we have had the CONVENTION HERALD published by H.E. Schmul of Salem, Ohio as the organ of the Interdenominational Holiness Convention, the umbrella organization for several of the very small splinter groups that have broken off from the various holiness churches.

Missions

The Holiness Movement has from the beginning had a strong missionary orientation, perhaps because it arose during the great century of missions and perhaps because of the influence of Acts 1:8 which conjoins the power of the Holy Spirit with witnessing to the end of the earth. Most denominations have their own board and missions program. The work of the Nazarenes has been described in a three volume work by Mendell Taylor, FIFTY YEARS OF NAZARENE MISSIONS (Kansas City, Mo.: Beacon Hill, 1952-1958) For the Pilgrims, innumerable small works describe specific fields, but the major survey is by Paul William Thomas, "An Historical Survey of Pilgrim World Missions." (Unpublished B.D. thesis, Asbury Theological Seminary. 1963) Byron S. Lamson has chronicled the work of the Free Methodists in VENTURE! THE FRONTIERS OF FREE METHODISM (Winona Lake, Ind.: Light and Life Press, 1960) Other material is described on pages 556-580 of Jones "Perfectionist

Persuasion" under the heading of the appropriate group. Current material usually may be found either in the denominational organ, or its missions magazine where that exists.

Two interdenominational mission boards have been associated with the holiness movement as a whole. Both date from the turn of the century. The first of these is the Oriental Mission Society founded in 1901 by Mr. and Mrs. Charles Cowman. Mrs. Lettie Burd Cowman is well known as the author of the widely read STREAMS IN THE DESERT, a devotional book. She also wrote a biography of her husband, CHARLES E. COWMAN, MISSIONARY WARRIOR (Los Angeles: Oriental Missionary Society · 1928) which serves as a major source for the early history of the OMS. There is also a biography of Mrs. Cowman by Benjamin H. Pearson, THE VISION LIVES (Los Angeles: Cowman Publications, 1961) More recently Edward and Esther Erny have written NO GUARANTEE BUT GOD: THE STORY OF THE FOUNDERS OF THE ORIENTAL MISSION- ARY SOCIETY (Greenwood, Ind.: Oriental Missionary Society. 1969) Current material is available in the ORIENTAL MISSIONARY STANDARD, organ of the OMS since 1901. OMS work is concentrated in South America as well as the Orient.

The second of these interdenominational boards, the National Holiness Missionary Society, was founded in 1910. The story of this organization was chronicled by W.W. Cary, STORY OF THE NATIONAL HOLINESS MISSIONARY SOCIETY (Chicago: National Holiness Missionary Society, 1940) Laura Cammack Trachsel picks up this story, now under the name World Gospel Mission, in three works, KINDLED FIRES IN AFRICA, KINDLED FIRES IN ASIA, and KINDLED FIRES IN LATIN AMERICA (Marion, Ind.: World Gospel Mission, 1960-1) Current material is available in CALL TO PRAYER, the organ of WGM since 1919.

Perhaps the term is too exalted, for although the
holiness movement has always drawn on the hymnody
of the whole church and especially the Wesleys,
the "gospel song" of the camp meeting is perhaps
most characteristic of the movement as a whole.
The impress of the camp meeting is still very much
felt. As nearly as I can determine this material
is to date little studied. The treatments that
are available deal with the camp meetings early in
the 19th century before the holiness revival or with
Ira Sankey of the Moody Revivals before the turn
of the next century. Some preliminary treatment
is found in Jones, "Perfectionist Persuasion."

Amazing numbers of gospel song hymnals for the use
of the holiness camp meetings were published during
the 19th century. Delbert Rose of Asbury maintains
a collection of several shelves for the CHA historical collection. A number of these were issued
under the auspices of the National Camp Meeting
Association. Among these are such titles as John
Inskip, SONGS OF TRIUMPH, ADAPTED TO PRAYER MEET-
INGS, CAMP MEETINGS AND ALL OTHER SEASONS OF
RELIGIOUS WORSHIP (Philadelphia: National Pub-
lishing Assn. for the Promotion of Holiness, 1882)
and William McDonald and Lewis Hortsough, BEULAH
SONGS: A CHOICE COLLECTION OF POPULAR HYMNS AND
MUSIC, NEW AND OLD, ESPECIALLY ADAPTED TO CAMP
MEETINGS, PRAYER AND CONFERENCE MEETINGS, FAMILY
WORSHIP AND ALL OTHER ASSEMBLIES WHERE JESUS IS
PRAISED (Philadelphia: National Association for
the Promotion of Holiness, 1879)   Similar is
William McDonald, et al., SONGS OF JOY AND GLADNESS
(Boston: McDonald & Gill, 1885) and Joshua Bill
and George A. McLaughlin, GOOD NEWS IN SONG
(Boston: The Christian Witness Co., 1891)   As
late as 1953, a similar title was published for
the use of the "Interdenominational Holiness
Movement" with an endorsement of the NHA Executive

Secretary, Dr. H.M. Couchenour. This was Kenneth
H. Wells, SONGS OF GRACE AND POWER (Chicago:
Evangel Mission Company, 1953)

The Nazarene Church perhaps has its roots most
directly in this tradition. Of particular signi-
ficance for them has been Haldor Lillenas, a con-
verted immigrant, who became a pastor and music
evangelist and established a music publishing
house that had great impact in the denomination.
His autobiography is available as DOWN MELODY LANE
(Kansas City. Mo.: Beacon Hill, 1953) and much
of his work can be found in the Nazarene hymnal,
PRAISE AND WORSHIP (Kansas City, Mo.: Lillenas
Pub. Co. n.d.), now being revised.

Most of the denominations now have their own
hymnals, often differing little from those of
larger denominations. One of the finest is a
joint effort by the Wesleyans and the Free Methodists, HYMNS OF THE LIVING FAITH (Marion, Ind.:
Wesleyan Methodist Publishing Assn., 1951 and
Winona Lake, Ind.: Light and Life Press, 1951),
now being revised, again by a joint committee.
Here one will find hymns by Phoebe Palmer, Haldor
Lillenas, and Ira Sankey with the finest efforts
of the whole Christian church.

Preaching

Much of the material cited above under "theology"
actually consisted originally of sermons and
addresses in churches or camp meetings. In addi-
tion certain collections of sermons have been compiled that can serve as illustrations of the
homiletical art of the holiness preachers. Again
available, though in mutilated form, is THE DOUBLE
CURE, OR ECHOES FROM NATIONAL CAMP MEETINGS
(Boston: McDonald and Gill, 1887 - the first 206
pages have been reprinted in paperback by Schmul,

47

1965) From the turn of the century we have THE
PENTECOSTAL PULPIT (Louisville: Pentecostal Pub-
lishing Co. n.d.) and TWENTIETH CENTURY HOLINESS
SERMONS (Louisville: Pentecostal Publishing Co., -
I have seen four printings and none carry a date)

In the twentieth century the Nazarenes have produced several items. First of these was THE
NAZARENE PULPIT (Kansas City, Mo.: Nazarene Publishing House, 1925) which contains thumbnail
sketches and photos of the preachers included.
More recently have appeared D. Shelby Corlett
(ed.) THE SECOND WORK OF GRACE (Kansas City, Mo.:
Beacon Hill, 1950) and James McGraw (ed.), THE
HOLINESS PULPIT (Kansas City. Mo.: Beacon Hill,
1957 Theologian Richard S. Taylor devoted his
most recent book to the topic PREACHING HOLINESS
TODAY (Kansas City. Mo.: Beacon Hill, 1968) which
originated in preaching seminars held at the NHA
annual conventions and is apparently designed for
his classes at the Nazarene Seminary. His bibliography (pp. 206-210) includes a list of holiness
sermons. Probably the most outstanding holiness
preacher today is Paul S. Rees, son of Seth Rees
and for years pastor of the First Covenant Church
of Minneapolis. From this period date THE FACT OF
OUR LORD (Grand Rapids: Eerdmans, 1951) and IF
GOD BE FOR US! (Grand Rapids: Eerdmans, 1940),
both of which went through several printings. More
recent books have consisted more of addresses or
biblical expositions.

I am aware of two magazines designed for preachers
within the holiness movement. For ten years (1949-
1958) W.C. Mavis of Asbury Seminary edited the
CHRISTIAN MINISTER, designed primarily for Free
Methodists. Still being published among the
Nazarenes (and founded in 1926) is the NAZARENE
PREACHER (Originally the PREACHER'S MAGAZINE)
The latter is more helpful, including among other
things theological articles and treatments of

various preachers important to the holiness tradition.

Historical Collections

Since I have done little archival work myself, I am here relying on the reports of those who have. For the 19th century one must turn primarily to the Methodist sources - the schools, the archives at the Methodist Historical Society at Lake Junaluska, N.C. and the Methodist Publishing House in Nashville. I am told that Drew's collection is particularly good in this area and what spot-checking I was able to do seems to confirm this. No doubt the UNION LIST OF METHODIST SERIALS and the METHODIST UNION CATALOG will be of great help in locating this material once they are published. The preliminary and checking editions serve somewhat in the meantime. Asbury has joined both of these and will list her collection there.

The archives and historical collection of the Christian Holiness Association are now in the hands of the official historian Dr Delbert Rose of Asbury Seminary and are stored for the present in the B.L. Fisher Library. Dr. Rose is currently producing from this material a history of the Association. His personal files also contain a great deal of interest. Asbury Theological Seminary has of course a significant collection, including files of the PENTECOSTAL HERALD, an index to Henry Clay Morrison's work therein, and an unorganized collection of the imprints of the Pentecostal Publishing Co. of Louisville. There are unfortunately many gaps.

As one moves out of the 19th century one must turn to the institutions or schools that have been produced by various facets of the movement. God's Bible School of Cincinnati has been associated with important figures, publishing and churches within the movement. Mention should perhaps also be made of Vennard College near Oskaloosa, Iowa (formerly the Chicago Evangelistic Institute) which is providing much of the CHRISTIAN WITNESS for ATLA filming.

Among the denominations, the Nazarenes have been perhaps the most assiduous. In 1955 they established a "Church History Commission" to collect the historical materials relating to the Nazarenes and to commission CALLED UNTO HOLINESS by Timothy Smith. He comments that nearly all the materials behind his book have been collected in Kansas City in the original or on microfilm. H.V. Synan comments in his dissertation, "The Pentecostal Movement in the United States," that this collection "constitutes the best source for manuscripts, periodicals, and general accounts relating to the National Holiness Movement and the holiness denominations which issued from it" (p. 277) I also understand that the collection at Pasadena College is particularly good and that Eastern Nazarene College has recently embarked on the development of a "holiness library" to collect at least the relevant books.

Most other holiness denominations have made some efforts to collect some materials. Bishop Leslie Marston has been engaged in this task for the Free Methodists. Some work has been done for the Wesleyans. The materials for the Church of God (Anderson, Ind.) have been collected in the Warner Memorial Collection of the School of Theology of Anderson College, Anderson, Indiana.

Recent Trends

Perhaps some recent trends and related bibliography would be of interest. I have held back some items that could have been mentioned earlier for treatment here.

1. Born in the forces of revivalism, the Holiness Movement still expects and sees God's power manifested in the "revival.   This has been particularly true of Asbury College where over the past twenty-five years there have been a number of "spontaneous revivals." The manifestations of 1950 and 1958 were chronicled in a booklet by Henry C. James and Paul Rader, HALLS AFLAME (Wilmore, Ky.: Asbury Seminary Press, 1959)   A much larger book tells the story of the events of the first week of February. 1970, and their impact on a wide number of colleges, churches and institutions, mostly within the holiness movement. The volume was edited by Robert E. Coleman of Asbury Theological Seminary as ONE DIVINE MOMENT (Old Tappan, N.J.: Revell, 1970)   Another contributor, Henry C. James, has maintained at Asbury Seminary a file of newspaper clippings, etc. associated with these events.

2. The holiness movement remains firmly evangelistic in nature. While most denominations are decreasing in membership, most holiness denominations are still vigorously growing. There is also a department of evangelism at Asbury Theological Seminary. The S.E. McCreless Chair of Evangelism is occupied by Robert E. Coleman who studied "Factors in the Expansion of the Methodist Episcopal Church from 1784 to 1812" (unpublished doctoral dissertation, University of Iowa, 1954) and applies his discoveries in such works as THE MASTER PLAN OF EVANGELISM (Westwood, N.J : Revell, 1964)   already translated into several languages, and DRY BONES CAN LIVE AGAIN: REVIVAL IN THE LOCAL CHURCH (Old Tappan, N.J.: Revell, 1969) The Nazarenes have produced a major work in this area by Mendell Taylor, EXPLORING EVANGELISM (Kansas City. Mo.: Beacon Hill, 1964)

3. The social concern of the original Wesleyan
    Revival and the mid-19th century revivals is
being recovered (not least because of pressure of
the younger generation!)   A department of church
and society has been established at Asbury Theological Seminary, and Gilbert James of that department has been the motivating force behind a new
"Urban Ministry Program for Seminarians" (UMPS) in
Chicago sponsored by a number of co-operating
seminaries and funded by the Lilly Foundation.
This concern has so far not produced any literature
other than a few essays in NHA collections about
to be mentioned.

4. Although denominations within the holiness
    movement consistently ignore the conciliar
movements on the national and international level,
they are fiercely ecumenical within their own
circle.   In 1966, some consideration was given to
turning the NHA into a federation of holiness
churches.   In the last very few years mergers have
produced both the Missionary Church and the
Wesleyan Church.   In its merging conference, the
Wesleyan Church voted to initiate discussions with
the Free Methodists.   These movements have been
studied by Howard A. Snyder, "Unity and the Holiness Churches" (B.D. thesis, Asbury Theological
Seminary. 1966)

5. Unfortunately the pattern of schism is just as
    firmly embedded in the tradition.   Mergers and
other forces have resulted in the formation of a
number of very small, conservative holiness denominations.   These include such groups as the
Allegheny Wesleyan Methodist Connection, the Bible
Missionary Church (originally Nazarene), the
Wesleyan Holiness Association (originally Bible
Missionary Church) the United Holiness Church and
the Evangelical Wesleyan Church (both originally
Free Methodist)   These groups are loosely grouped
today in the Inter-Denominational Holiness

Convention, which announced that 22 groups were participating in its 1971 Convention. This group is also now sponsoring a seminary of sorts, Aldersgate School of Religion, Hobe Sound, Florida. The IHC is being studied by David Webb of Asbury Seminary in a Th.M. thesis.

6. The 1960's have seen a renewed emphasis on scholarship. There has been founded a Wesleyan Theological Society that issues the WESLEYAN THEOLOGICAL JOURNAL now in its 6th volume (Spring, 1971), which publishes the papers of the annual November meetings. This joins the ASBURY SEMINARIAN (founded 1946), the only other theological journal in the movement. In the early 1960's the NHA sponsored a number of "doctrinal seminars" in which scholars within the movement read papers in the various educational institutions. These were collected by the president Kenneth Geiger, the motivating force behind the seminars, into three anthologies, INSIGHTS INTO HOLINESS (Kansas City, Mo.: Beacon Hill, 1962), FURTHER INSIGHTS INTO HOLINESS (Kansas City, Mo.: Beacon Hill, 1963), and THE WORD AND THE DOCTRINE (Kansas City, Mo.: Beacon Hill, 1965) Papers and addresses of the 1968 centennial convention of the NHA were collected as PROJECTING OUR HERITAGE (Kansas City. Mo.: Beacon Hill, 1969) edited by Myron F Boyd and Merne A. Harris.

7 For the most part holiness theology has remained unaffected by 20th century theological currents and turmoil. Some have suggested that in its harking back to Arminius as its theological forefather it might provide balancing emphases to some of the more extreme positions of modern neo-Reformation theology (cf. Carl Bangs, "Recent Studies in Arminianism," RELIGION IN LIFE, XXXII [Summer, 1963] p. 421) But so far no one has taken up the task of demonstrating this. Some within the tradition have been so bold as to

notice certain affinities within the movement to
at least some forms of existentialism (see, for
example, certain articles in the Spring-Summer,
1957 issue of the ASBURY SEMINARIAN)   One of
these, Nazarene theologian Mildred Bangs Wynkoop,
is seeing through the press what promises to be a
strikingly new interpretation of the Wesleyan
message, LOVE - THE DYNAMIC OF WESLEYANISM (to be
published in 1972 by Beacon Hill Press)   A section
of this appeared in the 1971 WESLEYAN THEOLOGICAL
JOURNAL. The present writer has been investigating
certain affinities between Wesley's SERMONS and
Sören Kiekegaard's STAGES ON LIFE'S WAY.

8.   But recent historical studies of the sources
     of the movement have been manifold. Many of
these have already been mentioned in the course of
the paper. One of the finest of these is by Free
Methodist George Turner of Asbury and is based on
his Harvard dissertation (1946)   This was published first as THE MORE EXCELLENT WAY (Winona
Lake: Light and Life Press, 1952) and has recently
been made available with some revision as THE
VISION WHICH TRANSFORMS (Kansas City, Mo.: Beacon
Hill, 1964 - reprinted 1970)   This volume treats
the biblical basis for perfection and traces the
concept through the whole history of the church
until the present day. Others start with Arminius
in finding theological foundations. Nazarene
Mildred Wynkoop has written FOUNDATIONS OF WESLEYAN-
ARMINIAN THEOLOGY (Kansas City, Mo.: Beacon Hill,
1967) and her brother Carl Bangs, formerly a
Nazarene and now a Methodist teaching at St. Paul
School of Theology. studied Arminius in his
University of Chicago doctoral program. Out of
this has come ARMINIUS: A STUDY IN THE DUTCH
REFORMATION to be published in June, 1971, by
Abingdon. Most writers start however with the
Wesleyan revival. One of the finest interpreta-
tions of this period has been by Free Methodist
Mary Alice Tenney of Greenville College, BLUEPRINT

FOR A CHRISTIAN WORLD (Winona Lake: Light and Life Press, 1953) Wesleyan Leo Cox has contributed JOHN WESLEY'S CONCEPT OF PERFECTION (Kansas City, Mo.: Beacon Hill, 1964) based on his Iowa dissertation (1959) We have already mentioned the efforts to tell the story of the American movement. A number of other such studies exist as dissertations but have not been published, and others are in process.

9. There has been a striking increase in biblical studies within the last few years. Two multivolume Bible commentaries have been produced. The Nazarenes produced the 10 volume BEACON BIBLE COMMENTARY (Kansas City. Mo.: Beacon Hill, 1964-69) A similar project, drawing on many of the same writers, has been edited by Charles W. Carter of Taylor University. the WESLEYAN BIBLE COMMENTARY (Grand Rapids: Eerdmans, 1964-69), six volumes in 7 parts (volume I having two sections) Dr. George Turner of Asbury Seminary attempted to draw on a larger community to produce an EVANGELICAL BIBLE COMMENTARY, modeled after the INTERPRETER'S BIBLE. This project collapsed after the appearance of the other two series, but nearly all the volumes produced were by holiness writers.[27] The

----

27. Directly in the series were Ralph Earle, THE GOSPEL ACCORDING TO MARK (Grand Rapids: Zondervan, 1957) Charles W. Carter and Ralph Earle, THE ACTS OF THE APOSTLES (Grand Rapids: Zondervan, 1959), George A. Turner and Julius R. Mantey. THE GOSPEL ACCORDING TO JOHN (Grand Rapids: Eerdmans, 1964) Intended for inclusion, but since published separately was the contribution of British Methodist C. Leslie Mitton, THE EPISTLE OF JAMES (Grand Rapids: Eerdmans, 1966) Other books, such as Turner on Hebrews, exist in manuscript and may yet see light in another form.

holiness schools have tended to perpetuate a
school of biblical interpretation called "Inductive
Bible Study" or "English Bible" developed primarily
at Biblical Seminary in New York City after the
turn of the century. The major text of this
approach is by Asbury Seminary's Dean Robert A.
Traina, formerly of Biblical, METHODICAL BIBLE
STUDY (latest printing available from the author,
Wilmore, Ky.) This approach was developed for
lay use in the Sunday Schools by Donald Joy (exec.
editor) ALDERSGATE BIBLICAL SERIES (published by
Light and Life Press of the Free Methodist Church)
The set of 40 volumes is still available and has
been used by a number of the holiness denominations, especially the Wesleyans and the Free
Methodists.

10. Finally. the movement has been influenced by
    the rise of psychology. Particular challen-
ges were raised by this area of study for a movement which has so emphasized Christian experience.
These men arose particularly among the Free Methodists. Bishop Leslie Marston made signal contributions in the field of psychology before turning
more to church work and the history of the denomination. He has also written FROM CHAOS TO CHARAC-
TER: A STUDY IN THE STEWARDSHIP OF PERSONALITY
(3rd ed., Winona Lake, Ind.: Light and Life Press,
1944) Orville S. Walters of the University of
Illinois has made contributions primarily in
journals in the field of psychiatry and also in
such publications as RELIGION IN LIFE. W. Curry
Mavis of Asbury Seminary has also produced several
books, most important of which has been the
PSYCHOLOGY OF CHRISTIAN EXPERIENCE (Grand Rapids:
Zondervan, 1963 - recently reissued in paperback)
The impact of such thinking has been to shift the
approach to Christian experience away from the
dogmatic patterns of the past to a more open,
need-oriented pattern of pastoral ministry.

Appendix I - Holiness Publishing

In the 19th century much holiness publishing was
done of course by the various Methodist publishing
houses. Books and tracts poured from the offices
of the GUIDE TO HOLINESS under several imprints.
The National Camp Meeting Association for the
Promotion of Holiness sponsored the National Publishing Association for the Promotion of Holiness,
located in Philadelphia. McDonald and Gill of
Boston, later of Chicago, took over the CHRISTIAN
WITNESS and under the imprint of the magazine became the major publisher by the turn of the
century.

Early in this century two midwest publishers became especially important. Martin W. Knapp founded
in Cincinnati what became the Revivalist Press and
was associated with GOD'S REVIVALIST and God's
Bible School. In Louisville, the Pentecostal
Publishing Company was associated with Henry Clay
Morrison and the Asbury institutions.

Later in this century the denominational houses
have come into prominence. The most prolific of
these has been the Nazarene Publishing House (including the Beacon Hill Press of Kansas City and
Lillenas Publishing Co., P.O. Box 527, Kansas City,
Mo. 64141)   Much recent CHA and movement wide
publishing has been done under the Beacon Hill
imprint. To a lesser extent and somewhat earlier
the Light and Life Press (Free Methodist Publishing House, Winona Lake, Ind. 46590) of the Free
Methodists made signal contributions. Other books
of interest outside the denominations involved
have been produced by the Wesley Press (Box 2000,
Marion, Indiana, 46952) of the Wesleyans and the
Warner Press (Box 2499, Anderson, Indiana, 46011)
of the Church of God (Anderson, Indiana)

The Revivalist Press (1810 Young Street,

Cincinnati, Ohio 45210) is still active and has been issuing a number of reprints. They moreover, handle other publishers and perhaps keep the best stock. Probably the most extensive reprinting program has been undertaken by H.E. Schmul, associated with the Inter-Denominational Holiness Convention (375 W. State St., Salem, Ohio 44460) His books are also sold through the Convention Book Club (Box 176, Cooperstown, Pa. 16317) Bethany Fellowship (6820 Auto Club Road, Minneapolis, Minnesota, 55431) has also reissued a few reprints as well as some important new books. A bookseller in Indiana specializes in the literature and has also produced a number of reprints (Newby Book Room, Rt. 1, Noblesville, Ind. 46060)

Appendix II - Other Addresses

Addresses, names of periodicals, etc. for the groups and mission boards mentioned in the above paper may be found in such standard sources as the WORLD CHRISTIAN HANDBOOK (1968) and the YEARBOOK OF AMERICAN CHURCHES (1971) with the following exceptions and changes:

1. The Christian Holiness Association must be sought under its old name, the National Holiness Association.

2. The Oriental Missionary Society
   Box A (1200 Fry Road)
   Greenwood, Indiana 46142

3. The Evangelical Church of North America has its headquarters at 7733 West River Road North, Minneapolis, Minnesota, 55430, also the address of its organ, THE EVANGELICAL ADVOCATE.

4. The EVANGELICAL FRIEND of The Evangelical
    Friends Alliance is published and edited
    at 600 East Third Street (P.O. Box 232)
    Newberg, Oregon 97123.

5. Rocky Mountain Yearly Meeting of the
       Friends Church
    2610 East Bijou Street
    Colorado Springs, Colorado 80909

www.ingramcontent.com/pod-product-compliance
Lightning Source LLC
Chambersburg PA
CBHW020521030426
42337CB00011B/497